THE TRUTH IS

1. Leveling up your craft to write a story that lives long after you've left the planet is what some might call a ridiculous goal.

2. You will not tell that story after reading just one how-to-write book.

3. You will not tell that story as the result of taking one seminar.

4. You know creating a timeless work of art will require the dedication of a world-class athlete. You will be training your mind with as much ferocity and single-minded purpose as an Olympic gold medal hopeful. That kind of cognitive regimen excites you, but you just haven't found a convincing storytelling dojo to do that work.

5. The path to leveling up your creative craft is a dark and treacherous one. You've been at it a long time, and it often feels like you're wearing three-dimensional horse blinders. More times than you'd like to admit, you're not sure if you're moving north or south or east or west. And the worst part? You can't see anyone else, anywhere, going through what you're going through. You're all alone.

WELCOME TO THE STORY GRID UNIVERSE

HERE'S HOW WE CONTEND WITH THOSE TRUTHS

1. We believe we find meaning in the pursuit of creations that last longer than we do. This is *not* ridiculous. Seizing opportunities and overcoming obstacles as we stretch ourselves to reach for seemingly unreachable creations is transformational. We believe this pursuit is the most valuable and honorable way to spend our time here. Even if—especially if—we never reach our lofty creative goals.

2. Writing just one story isn't going to take us to the top. We're moving from point A to Point A^{5000}. We've got lots of mountains to climb, lots of rivers and oceans to cross, and many deep dark forests to traverse along the way. We need topographic guides, and if they're not available, we'll have to figure out how to write them ourselves.

3. We're drawn to seminars to consume the imparted wisdom of an icon in the arena, but we leave with something far more valuable than the curriculum. We get to meet the universe's other pilgrims and compare notes on the terrain.

4. The Story Grid Universe has a virtual dojo, a university in which to work out and get stronger—a place to stumble, correct mistakes, and stumble again, until the moves become automatic and mesmerizing to outside observers.

5. The Story Grid Universe has a performance space, a publishing house dedicated to leveling up the craft with clear boundaries of progress and the ancillary reference resources to pack for each project mission. There are an infinite number of paths to where you want to be, with a story that works. Seeing how others have made it down their own yellow-brick roads to release their creations into the timeless creative cosmos will help keep you on the straight and narrow path.

All are welcome—the more, the merrier. But please abide by the golden rule:

Put the work above all else, and trust the process.

THE STORY MICROSCOPE

THE SURPRISING WAY A SPREADSHEET CAN SAVE YOUR MANUSCRIPT

KIMBERLY KESSLER

STORY GRID

STORY GRID

Story Grid Publishing LLC
223 Egremont Plain Road
PMB 191
Egremont, MA 01230

First Story Grid Publishing Paperback Edition
June 2021

For Information about Special Discounts for Bulk
Purchases,
Please visit www.storygridpublishing.com

ISBN: 978-1-64501-071-5
Ebook: 978-1-64501-073-9

For

All Past, Present, and Future Story Nerds

ABOUT THIS BOOK

Congratulations. You've poured your heart out onto the page, bled yourself dry, and created a first draft. But before your story is ready to delight your readers, this beautiful heap of words needs to be read, evaluated, and revised.

Or maybe you're not through the first draft stage. Maybe you're still entertaining the inklings of an idea and getting to know your genre through stories you love and want to emulate.

Either way, the next step is to look closely at how to put a story together from the ground up.

Imagine if you had a tool that allowed you to take in an entire story at a glance. You could see how all of the scenes in the story relate to each other and identify the critical components that have the biggest impact on whether the story works for the reader.

This may be surprising, but it turns out the most underrated tool for telling a powerful story is a spreadsheet.

If you have experience using spreadsheets, you might already appreciate the value of laying thoughts out on a grid. If that's not you, and the thought of parsing through prose to fill in a spreadsheet creates a sense of unease, fear not. Using a spreadsheet will not reduce the story you love into meaningless ones and zeroes.

If you associate spreadsheets with numbers and accounting, set that aside as we take a look at how spreadsheets can work with words to help us tell powerful stories. In fact, I believe the methodical ritual of filling in a spreadsheet allows us to access a special kind of magic. When we commit to the process and dig into the details of the story, the muse grants us access to a deeper understanding of what the story really means.

Even if you don't believe in the muse or magic, the process is still powerful because when you get down to it, a spreadsheet is simply a structured way of taking notes. We can use it for words and concepts just as easily as for numbers and math.

In this book, I'll take you through how to fill in and analyze the Story Grid Spreadsheet. First, we'll go over when to use the spreadsheet and how to set it up. Once you've prepared your spreadsheet, we'll walk through the specific process for finding the information you need and filling it in. You'll learn what information goes into each cell and how it contributes to telling a great story. Finally, we'll explore the ways you can use your spreadsheet to discover insights about the story.

Regardless of your current level of experience, I encourage you to lean into the gridded layout of the spreadsheet and experience what commitment to the process can do for you. You'll be amazed at how understanding the basics of the Story Grid Spreadsheet will improve your understanding of story. With practice and time, you can level up bit by bit and unlock even deeper insights. Doing this work will make you a better storyteller—the strangest magic of all.

THE STORY GRID SPREADSHEET: UNDERSTANDING THE GRID

To get the most out of your spreadsheeting experience, it helps to understand the features that make this tool so useful for evaluating stories.

When we fill in a spreadsheet, we enter information into cells, which are the individual boxes. The cells are grouped into rows, which are horizontal lines of cells identified using numbers, and columns, which are vertical lines of cells identified using letters. We can put any information we want into the cells, and later on we can sort, compare, and even graph the information along its rows and columns.

But what makes it such a great tool for understanding stories? It boils down to two things.

    1. Objectivity. To fill in the spreadsheet one cell at a time, you have to

narrow your focus. Each cell poses a specific question. The cell's column specifies a particular kind of information, and the row specifies a particular search area within the story (a scene). You have to go to the pages of the scene to find the specific answer. If you can't find the answer on the page, it doesn't get to go on the sheet. This specificity makes us confront our assumptions and stay objective.

2. Connection. When we see the information in the cells displayed together, we can mentally zoom in and out to view the story on different levels. The grid structure helps us see how the information works together. Within a row, we can see how different aspects of the scene contribute to the scene as a whole. Within a column, we can examine a scene's role in the entire story. When the grid makes these relationships explicit, we can evaluate connections that we might miss without the structure of the spreadsheet.

By examining a story scene by scene and

logging it on a super nerdy spreadsheet, we can see more clearly what is actually on the page—and what is not. Then, we can make better sense of what is working—and what is not. Ultimately, we can decide what to change. Knowledge and clarity empower us to make intentional creative choices about our own work and tell better stories.

WHEN TO USE THE SPREADSHEET (AND WHEN NOT TO)

The Story Grid Spreadsheet helps us evaluate the full text of an existing story, whether it's a draft we've finished or a masterwork we want to study to improve our craft. It is not intended to be a planning tool for the first draft. When you're planning a story, you'll consider some of the same information that goes into the spreadsheet because it contains the essential components of a story that works. Before you start to write a scene, it's useful to know where you're starting (when and where it takes place) and where you're going (what you want to happen and how it could affect the global arc).

It may be tempting to chart every scene on your spreadsheet ahead of time so you have a specific map for your draft, but the level of detail the spreadsheet captures is more likely to stifle your creativity than fuel it. (And I say this as a hardcore outliner.)

Writing is a different cognitive process than editing. When you are writing, you are creating new realities. It's important that your mind is free to jump and flow to capture the raw essence of an idea or moment—the feeling of the experience as it happens. This is true whether you outline your story before drafting or not. Drafting is all about being present and tapping into the freedom to express what comes up.

When editing, you are observing the reality you created. This is a great time to fill in the spreadsheet. It will help you take a step back from your work so you can identify what isn't working in your story and revise with intention.

If you are evaluating a work in progress, you can ground yourself in the spreadsheet's ability to distance you from the work so you can see what is on the page rather than assuming you've written what you intended. Ultimately, this will help you tell the story you want to tell.

When studying a story that inspires you, you're there to observe and learn so you can achieve a deeper understanding of what makes the story you love stand the test of time as a go-to example of its genre. This masterwork becomes a model you can apply to your own work in progress.

Whether you choose to dive into a masterwork or a work in progress, the process will be the same. Either way, focusing on what you want to accomplish by completing the spreadsheet will help you stay focused.

2

PREPPING ALL THE PIECES

Before you jump into analyzing, you must get a few proverbial ducks in a row (and column).

THE BOOK

As you fill in your spreadsheet, you'll need a copy of the story close at hand. The clues to everything you need are in the text. All you need to do is look closely.

The way you take notes will vary depending on whether you're reading a digital or physical copy, and whether it's a masterwork or a work in progress. For a digital masterwork, like an ebook, use highlights and comments to make notes in the scene. For a digital work in progress, like a Word document, use highlights and comments as well as bold, italics, and underlines. For a print copy of a masterwork or work in progress, you can use pens, pencils, colored pencils, highlighters, sticky notes, or even index cards. Pick the most useful method for you.

THE SHEET

To get started, you need a blank spreadsheet with headings for the columns you will use to track your scenes. We can break fourteen columns into four groups according to the purpose of the information they track. Each column is important to the analysis because it tracks a specific piece of information that is essential to the story.

At Story Grid, we are committed to leveling up our craft, just like you are. Our tools evolve over time to reflect our deeper understanding of Story.

In this book, you'll learn the fundamentals of the Story Grid Spreadsheet. The examples are based on a fourteen-column layout. We regularly update this format, but the principles you'll learn in this book still apply. To see the current format of the Spreadsheet, check out the template available here https://storygrid.com/beats/spreadsheet/.

Analytical Constraints or Tracking the Global Story: In *The Story Grid*, Shawn Coyne calls this Tracking the Global Story because these columns are an inventory of the scenes in the story. We'll track fourteen columns in the spreadsheet. I like to use the term Analytical Constraints because when we're completing these columns, we are narrowing the scope of the text to precisely what we want to examine for that scene.

- Scene Number
- Word Count
- Story Event

Change: What is different at the beginning of the scene versus the end of the scene?

- Value Shift
- Polarity Shift
- Turning Point

Continuity: Who is telling the story? When and where does the scene take place?

- Point of View
- Period/Time
- Duration
- Location

Characters: Who populates the scene?

- Onstage Characters
- Number of Onstage Characters

- Offstage Characters
- Number of Offstage Characters

You have a couple of options when setting up a spreadsheet with these columns.

If you want to create a spreadsheet from scratch, you can use software such as Excel, Numbers, or Google Sheets. Open a new, blank spreadsheet in the program of your choice and populate the first row of each of the fourteen columns, one heading per column. That's really all you need to begin!

Your other option is the Story Grid Spreadsheet template. This Google Sheets template has all of the scene-specific columns laid out, along with a few more that situate the scene within the overall arc of the story. Dropdown menus help you fill in the cells. The template also connects the spreadsheet to other Story Grid tools.

You can access the Story Grid Spreadsheet template on the resources page at https://storygrid.com/beats/spreadsheet/.

THE PROCESS

Once your spreadsheet is set up, it's time to fill it in. You need to capture a lot of details for each scene. Instead of trying to find all the information in one read, we're going to break it up into three distinct passes. In each pass, you'll have a different focus that will help you find the information you need to fill in a set of the cells in the spreadsheet.

The *first pass* is to get your bearings in the story and define where the scene begins and ends so you can fill in the information for Analytical Constraints or Tracking the Global Story.

The *second pass* focuses on the details that help the reader understand the world of the story. You will find specific indicators of time and space and concrete identifiers for characters to fill in the scene's Continuity and Characters information.

The *third pass* explores the beating heart of the scene. Change—the reason the reader comes to a story in the first place.

Each pass consists of three steps: *reading*, *finding*, and *filling*.

- **Reading:** For each pass, you will read the scene with a focus on specific information in the text. Don't try to go from memory. Read it fresh each time.
- **Finding:** Identify the text that gives you the specific information you need to fill in the cells you are working on. It's important to

evaluate *what's on the page* instead of getting lured away by your subjective experience or, if it's a draft, your intention. Marking the specific text that tells you each piece of information will keep you focused on what is on the page. Annotate, highlight, or underline the text.

- **Filling:** Review your annotations and complete each cell the best you can. Make notes for things that are missing or incomplete. Remember, even masterworks can have scenes with issues.

When you've completed this process for each scene in the story, your Story Grid Spreadsheet is complete.

Now, the time has come to roll up your sleeves and dig in for yourself. You're going to peel back the layers of each scene one by one. Like doing anything for the first time, it's going to feel a little strange and off balance. Just go with it. The steps laid out in the coming chapters will walk you through exactly what to do and in what order. Your job is to lean in.

3

FIRST PASS: DEFINING THE SCENE

In your first pass, you are reading for broad content and to get a feel for the story.

The goal is to experience what happens in the story the way a reader would while gaining an understanding of where the scene begins and ends on the page.

You may be wondering, *How will I know where a scene begins and ends?* For this first pass, just follow your gut instinct. Where does it feel like the scene you want to analyze begins and ends? Go ahead and call that a scene.

Surprised? Don't be.

This gut-level process is not easy to describe, but it's something you have whether you know it or not. You are human and have a sense of story in your DNA. Use it. Just do your best and get moving. You can always tweak it later.

When you have identified where the scene

begins and ends, it's time to start a row for that scene on your spreadsheet. On your first pass, you'll fill in the information for Analytical Constraints or Tracking the Global Story: Scene Number, Word Count, and a placeholder for the Story Event.

SCENE NUMBER

The scene number is precisely what it sounds like—a sequence of numbers (1, 2, 3) to identify each scene. This not only makes the story organized and easy to reference but serves as a tool for gauging the pace and flow of the narrative. You will be able to see where, when, and how often other data comes up in the story.

WORD COUNT

Word Count is (no surprise) the number of words that make up the range of text you have identified as the scene you want to analyze. This is an indicator of the amount of time it will take the reader to experience this portion of the story. When analyzing a film, you can use the timestamps to measure the amount of time each scene lasts. When analyzing a comic book or graphic novel, you can use the number of pages or panels. The point is to recognize the relative length of the scene to understand the timing of various aspects of the story, so use what makes sense for the medium.

To find the word count in a print book or ebook, we get to do a little math.

- Find the average words per line. Count the number of words in each line of a paragraph and find the average.
- Count the total number of lines for a full page.
- Multiply the average number of words per sentence by the total lines per full page. This will yield the average words per page.
- Then, to find the word count for the scene, count the number of pages in the scene. Pay attention to partial and blank pages for the most accurate estimate.
- Multiply the number of pages in the scene by the average words per page. This will give you the approximate word count for the scene.

STORY EVENT (PLACEHOLDER)

For the first pass, the Story Event is a

simple description of what happens in the scene. Fill in the cell with a placeholder to remind you what the scene is about. You can revise this in the third pass once you know more about the scene, but for now just jot down what stands out to you most about it. This will anchor your thoughts as you complete the rest of the analysis for the scene.

CRAFTING STRONGER STORIES BY TRACKING THE GLOBAL STORY

By identifying the boundaries of our scenes, we set expectations for how often we should see movement in the story. Stories don't happen all at once. Rather, they unfold moment by moment. A compelling narrative has movement throughout the entire story, which creates pacing that keeps the reader engaged.

Imagine a three-minute song that opens with a lively melody, only for the remaining two and a half minutes to be one unchanging note. Most boring song ever! Or, on the flip side, imagine it begins with one unchanging note, only to kick up an epic chorus for the last thirty seconds. Either way, no one is sticking around to hear that whole song.

The same is true for stories. We want to *feel* the arc—a captivating hook, progressive build, and harrowing payoff. Writers create this feeling by crafting smaller shifts that build into larger ones. This engages the audience and keeps them reading (or watching or listening).

The spreadsheet helps us to see whether this movement is happening in each scene. When you fill in the information for Analytical Constraints or Tracking the Global Story and determine where a scene begins and ends, you define a space within the story in which you expect to see movement.

FIRST PASS SUMMARY

- **Reading:** Begin reading from the beginning of the book or from the end of the previous scene. Use your story instincts to determine when enough has happened that it feels like a scene.
- **Finding:** Determine the word count for that section of text.
- **Filling:** Complete the first three columns on the spreadsheet for Scene Number, Word Count, and a placeholder Story Event that reminds you what the scene is about.

4

SECOND PASS: CONNECTING TO THE PAGE

The second time you read through the scene, you're looking at the text more closely to find clues that point to Continuity and Characters. These details orient the reader in time and space and help them understand who is in the scene. With this information, the reader can make sense of the moment and how it relates to all that came before. Consistency in these details protects the reader's experience because they disengage from the story when they notice errors. If they can stay immersed, they can focus on what the story is really about.

As you read, mark (bold, underline, italicize, or add a comment to) the text that reveals the time or location of the scene, denotes the passage of time, or refers to a character or the storyteller. As you look for supporting text for the Continuity information, you may find several clues that together inform you of the contents of any one of the cells.

When you have completed your pass and inline notations, review the text you marked and fill in the Continuity and Characters information.

POINT OF VIEW

This is where we identify the narrator who is telling the story in this particular scene. The choice and execution of the point of view directly shapes the way the story is told and impacts the reader's experience.

When you fill in the Point of View for each scene, include the following details:

- Perspective (first, second, or third person)
- Level of omniscience
- Narrator's name, if known
- Tense (past, present, future)
- Whether the story is being shown or told
- If applicable, explicit narrative devices (for example, a scene told in letters)

The Point of View cell for each scene of

Jane Eyre by Charlotte Bronte could read like this:

> First person for Jane Eyre
> Telling in Past Tense
> Written account, autobiography
> addressed to the reader

As you read, look for clues to the different aspects of the point of view. The pronouns used to refer to characters reveal whether the scene is in first person, second person, or third person. Look at verb tenses as well. Are they in past, present, or future tense? Content such as sensory descriptions or inner thoughts are clues to what information is available to the narrator and show whether they are operating with omniscience or have limited perspective.

For more detailed information about the components of point of view, check out *Point of View: Why Narrative Perspective Can Make or Break Your Story* by Leslie Watts.

PERIOD/TIME

This is where you track *when* the scene takes place. It could be the year, season, month, day, or time of day. Look for concrete details in the text that point to Period/Time, either overtly or covertly.

Here is an example from the opening chapter of *Jane Eyre* by Charlotte Bronte. The bolded words are all clues about Period/Time:

Folds of scarlet drapery shut in my view to the right hand; to the left were the clear panes of glass, protecting, but not separating me from the drear **November day**. At intervals, while turning over the leaves of my book, I studied the aspect of that **winter afternoon**.

Depending on the level of information on the page, you may find different levels of specificity in each scene.

DURATION

This is where you track (or estimate) how much time passes in the story during the scene: number of years, months, weeks, days, hours, or minutes. It works hand in hand with Period/Time to demonstrate how the story is moving forward through time and helps the reader make sense of what's happening.

Look for concrete details in the text that point to the passage of time, either overtly or covertly. Here is the opening paragraph of *Jane Eyre* as an example:

There was no possibility of taking a walk that **day**. We had been wandering, indeed, in the leafless shrubbery **an hour in the morning**; but **since dinner** (Mrs. Reed, when there was no company, dined **early**) the cold winter wind had brought with it clouds so sombre, and a rain so penetrating, that further outdoor exercise was now out of the question.

Later in the chapter, Jane mentions it's the afternoon, so we can deduce that about six to eight hours have passed so far in the story.

LOCATION

This is *where* the events of the scene take place. This column, along with Period/Time, orients the reader in the reality genre of the story and establishes expectations for what is believable or not. A space station sets very different expectations from what we expect in a brothel... not to mention an intergalactic brothel on a space station!

Look for concrete details in the text that point to location—either overtly or covertly.

Ready Player One by Ernest Cline is an interesting case study for location because the protagonist is often in two relevant locations simultaneously: the real world and the virtual world known as the OASIS.

> I fell out of my folding chair and landed with a thud on **the floor of my hideout**. My OASIS console tracked this movement and attempted to make my avatar drop to **the floor of my Latin classroom**, but the classroom conduct software prevented it from moving and a warning flashed on my display: PLEASE REMAIN SEATED DURING CLASS!

A scene may have multiple locations. Fill in the location information with a list of the specific places the characters in the scene visit.

ONSTAGE AND OFFSTAGE CHARACTERS

As you read, highlight any text that identifies a character or group of characters. This may be a name (e.g., Jane Eyre), a profession (the cook), or a descriptor (the boy with one leg).

Note that characters may be referred to more than once and by more than one identifier. For example, in the opening scene of *Jane Eyre,* the characters refer to Jane in three different ways on the page: I, Jane, Janet.

While reading the scene, feel free to highlight as many as you'd like, but then consolidate your thoughts so you count the character just once.

Before completing the cells within these columns, you need to determine whether each one you highlighted is truly a character and whether they are onstage or offstage. Let's look at how to make these distinctions.

Determining Characters and Non-Characters

For the most part, characters are going to be obvious. In most circumstances, a person—whether they are described with a proper noun or not—is a character. This includes the dead, undead, spirits, monsters, and animals.

However, sometimes it's not clear. The text might reference a historical person or quote an author who never appears in the story. As you consider whether to track these people, think about whether they have an impact on the scene. Are they capable of being active and making choices? Or are they only capable of being acted upon, like an element of the setting?

It's also useful to consider their purpose in the scene and their influence on the other characters. A corpse lying in a casket may not have agency, but their influence on the characters around them is certainly worth tracking.

At rare times, an object is a character.

In *The Lord of the Rings*, the One Ring may be an object, but it displays agency by choosing and acting on its own free will. The One Ring always wants to get back to its master and will betray its bearer.

In *Stranger Than Fiction*, Harold Crick's watch is constantly trying to get Harold's attention, and in the end, it sacrifices itself to save his life.

In the end, you decide what is most useful for you to track.

Determining Onstage and Offstage Characters

Onstage characters are those who physically appear in the scene. Offstage characters are those who do not physically appear in the scene but are mentioned by the narrator or onstage characters. There are a few considerations to note when making this distinction.

If a character comes onstage at any point in the scene, consider them onstage. For example, a character who is mentioned offstage at first and enters the scene later is onstage.

If a character is only thought about or

mentioned by others, consider them offstage. When another character is reliving a memory, an offstage character may have lines of dialogue, but they are not really part of the scene taking place. Consider them offstage.

At times a flashback or dream can feel like a scene. If it's useful to you, you may want to track it as its own scene on the spreadsheet so you can distinguish it from other scenes. Again, it's up to you to make a judgment call on how you are going to treat the characters.

Onstage Characters

Once you've determined which individuals and groups are truly characters that physically appear in the scene, fill in the cell with a list of at least one name or identifying word/phrase for each. You may choose to list their additional identifiers for reference, such as Jane (Janet).

Offstage Characters

Just as with onstage characters, we'll track these by making a list in the spreadsheet cell of the names/identifiers of each offstage character or group of characters.

Number of Onstage and Offstage Characters

These columns track the total number of characters in each category (onstage and offstage), whether individuals or groups, who appear in the scene.

When determining whether to count a group as one character or its total number (either exact or estimated based on the context), consider how the group functions in the scene. Is it referred to and acting as a singular entity? For example, a mob moves together and makes choices as a unit. Count these groups as one character.

A group might also act as a collective of individuals with separate and distinct agency. Pay attention to whether the individual members of a group make distinct choices. Count these groups according to the distinct characters within the group. In *The Lord of the Rings*, the fellowship is a group but made of nine individuals who demonstrate distinct agency, so each would be counted separately. A group of orcs, on the other hand, operate as a unit and may be best counted as one character.

CRAFTING STRONGER STORIES THROUGH CONTINUITY AND CHARACTERS

Together, the Continuity and Character columns track essential items the reader uses to make sense of the story. Having clear details in the text anchors the reader in time and space so they can follow the movement of the characters easily. When these details are consistent, the narrative flows and the reader is able to suspend their disbelief and stay immersed in the story.

The Character columns track the comings and goings of each character. At a glance, you can see when they first appear, how often they appear, and their final appearance. This information is an asset and allows you to identify characters who "fall off the page" by going unmentioned for too long, or appear once and are never mentioned again.

You can also keep track of how big the cast of each scene is. The Character columns show you how many characters the reader has to manage in their mind at one time, so you can avoid overwhelming them with too many characters or constricting your world with too few. Ensuring that you mention offstage characters adds a dimension of authenticity by making the world larger than just who is onstage at any given time.

Continuity and Character information helps you to maximize the potency of the reader's experience by maintaining clarity, managing pacing, and paying off expectations.

SECOND PASS SUMMARY

- **Reading:** As you read the scene again, pay close attention to on-the-page details.
- **Finding:** Mark any text that signals the point of view, period/time, duration, location, and characters. Assess the details you've marked. Is there enough information on the page for a reader to understand the point of view, period/time, duration, and location? Determine if the character names and descriptions you marked are truly characters, and if so, whether they are onstage or offstage. Count the characters in each group.
- **Filling:** Enter your conclusions into the cells for each Continuity and Character column. Leave blanks and make notes to yourself for things that are missing or incomplete.

5

THIRD PASS: FINDING THE PULSE

In the third pass, dig deeper into the beginning, middle, and end that you felt in your first read.

When you sense the arc of a story or scene, you are intuitively identifying a change taking place in the life of the character. Because we want readers to connect with our stories, the changes we track correspond to universal human experience. The fundamental aspects of existence that we use to identify the change in a story are called values, and they are tightly linked to universal human needs.

Abraham Maslow defined universal needs when he created his hierarchy of needs. At the foundation, the most primal need is physiological survival (air, water, and shelter). After that are the needs for safety (physical and psychological), love (relationships and belonging), esteem (recognition and respect), self-actualization (personal growth), and self-transcendence (contributing to something greater than yourself). This list of needs taps into every human experience and, because stories exist to help us make sense of life and solve problems, every story will tie back to at least one of these needs. Each genre has a core need that primarily drives the story forward, but at the scene level, change can impact any of the basic human needs.

The change in state of a human need can be represented along a spectrum of value that spans from a completely *unmet* need to the need being completely *met*, and every state in between. We use words and phrases to describe this spectrum of value as accurately as we can.

When we analyze a scene, we look for how the values for the characters have changed. We can differentiate several aspects of change: what changed (Value Shift), how it changed (Polarity Shift) and in which moment it changed (Turning Point).

As you read, look for indicators in the text that give you this information. You can use the Story Grid Scene Analysis Questions and the Five Commandments to help you determine the change in a scene.

STORY GRID SCENE ANALYSIS QUESTIONS

1. What are the characters literally doing—that is, what are their micro on-the-surface actions?
2. What is the essential tactic of the characters—that is, what above-the-surface macro behaviors are they employing that are linked to a universal human value?
3. What beyond-the-surface universal human values have changed for one or more characters in the scene? Which one of those value changes is most important and should be included in the Story Grid Spreadsheet?
4. The Scene Event Synthesis: What Story Event sums up the scene's on-the-surface, above-the-surface, and beyond-the-surface change? We will enter that event in the Story Grid Spreadsheet.

The Five Commandments

1. What is the Inciting Incident?
2. What is the Turning Point Progressive Complication?

3. What is the Crisis?
4. What is the Climax?
5. What is the Resolution?

Using your answers to these questions, you can fill in the information for the Change of the scene.

VALUE SHIFT

In the cells of this column, you will describe "what changed" in the scene. More specifically, you will note the most relevant and important change that occurs. Using two words or phrases, you will demonstrate the change by identifying the character's place on the value spectrum before and after the change. For example, you might identify a shift from *Hopeful* to *Hopeless*.

To make this as useful to your analysis as possible, you want to be intentional about the words you use. As you describe your value shifts, ask yourself if you can get more specific by using one or more of the following strategies.

Paired Shift

First and foremost, the two values you choose should exist within the same value spectrum to depict a change about a specific quality of life. For example, *Hungry* to *Fed* makes sense because they are both about food and sustaining your life, but *Hungry* to *Recognized* wouldn't because the words are not on the same spectrum of value. They are not related to the same need.

Relevant Shift

Once you've determined that your beginning and ending values are present on the same spectrum, consider whether that spectrum is the most relevant one for your story. For example, in the global inciting incident of a Love story, the lovers meet. The nature of this scene means the lovers will invariably shift from something like *Unknown* to *Known*, or *Strangers* to *Acquaintances*, or even *Never Met* to *Met*. But that doesn't really tell us the quality of the meeting. Something like *Ignorance* to *Attraction* or *Ignorance* to *Repulsion* does a little more in that it shows us how the lovers feel after having met, and it links their meeting back to the global genre.

Nuanced Shift

When you have a value shift that occurs along a relevant spectrum of value, consider whether you can be more specific and find nuances that help your analysis process. We want to beware of tracking every scene with one-note value shifts because it limits your ability to assess global progressive complications and irreversibility. So, while you could track every scene that turns on the global value spectrum in a "she loves me... she loves me not... she loves me..." kind of way, you can deepen your analysis by using more specific words that express smaller increments of change and have connotations that express the particular quality of your story.

For example, the scene where the lovers meet could be valued as *Ignorance* to *Attraction*, but other words could tell us more about the underlying meaning of the change:

- *Bored* to *Piqued*
- *Resigned* to *Hopeful*
- *Despairing* to *Enamored*

Each of these evokes different scenes and circumstances for the characters, which can be useful later during analysis and revisions.

POLARITY SHIFT

This is where we identify "how the value changed" or the direction of change. Is the need closer to being met or further from being met by the end of the scene than it was at the beginning?

To determine the direction of change along the value spectrum, look at the word or phrase you've chosen to represent the beginning and ending value states. How would you rank the value along the spectrum of need? Is it closer to their need being met or closer to being unmet?

A met need is considered positive, or +.
An unmet need is considered negative, or -.
If a scene begins positive but ends negative, it would be shown as + to -.
If a scene begins negative but ends positive, it would be shown as - to +.
Our example of *Hungry* to *Fed* would be a negative to a positive change, - to +.

If a scene begins with a positive value and ends with a positive value, ask yourself if the ending value is more positive than the beginning value. This would be shown as + to ++. The same would go for a scene that begins negative and ends negative. Is the ending state more negative than the opening state? This would be shown as - to --. These shifts are less common but do occur.

The four directions of change you would typically show are:

- - / + for negative to positive
- + / - for positive to negative
- - / -- for negative to double negative
- + / ++ for positive to double positive

Above all, it's important when evaluating the scene to discern whether the beginning and ending states are different enough. This is not to say that every scene must include a large shift. On the contrary, subtle shifts have the potential to build beautiful arcs of change across the larger units of story. But if the beginning and ending states are basically the same, nothing has changed. A scene that doesn't change doesn't work.

TURNING POINT

This is where we identify "where change happens" in the scene. To be clear, change will (or should) be happening at various points across the scene, but the Turning Point Progressive Complication is the key moment of change. This fulcrum shifts the values.

In the cells of this column, use a sentence to pinpoint this moment, and classify it as an active or revelatory moment.

- Active Turning Points happen when the value shifts because an unexpected event occurs "on location," enacted by a character or an aspect of the environment. It's a physical change.
- Revelatory Turning Points happen when the value shifts because new information enters the picture, either from a character or the environment, or because the protagonist gains a new perspective on information they already know. It's a mental change.

STORY EVENT (REVISITED)

Now that you've completed the scene analysis, you can update the Story Event column with your new and improved sentence that sums up the on-the-surface, above-the-surface, and beyond-the-surface change that (hopefully) happens in the scene.

If there is no perceivable change in the scene or if the change is ineffective, highlight the cells and/or make notes to yourself to that effect.

CRAFTING STRONGER STORIES THROUGH CHANGE

Without change, there is no story. It's vital that you can identify the specific text that communicates the change on the page. This ensures the reader can understand the change, which is fundamental to their experience of the story. Moments of change, when values shift, evoke an emotion in the reader. When different universal human needs are on the line in a story, we are hardwired to feel a certain way.

Whether readers know it or not, this feeling is why they read and what they ultimately want, so let's make sure each scene delivers. That means we don't want just *any* change to happen in the scene. The change must contribute to the greater whole—the global story experience of the reader. So even when you identify a change happening in the scene, that may not mean the scene is working for the story. This is something you may not be able to see clearly until you've finished the spreadsheet.

Once your spreadsheet is complete, you can use the Change columns to see the shift that happens (or doesn't happen) in each scene, as well as how sequences of scenes build to bigger changes across larger units of story.

THIRD PASS SUMMARY

- **Reading:** Read the scene again in full.
- **Finding:** Use the Story Grid Scene Analysis Questions and the Five Commandments to pinpoint the most relevant change that takes place in the scene.
- **Filling:** Using what you've found, fill in the Value Shift, Polarity Shift, and Turning Point information. Then revise your placeholder Story Event with your synthesis of the scene.

6

MAKING SENSE OF WHAT YOU FOUND

Even when you've finished filling in the spreadsheet, you may still have blanks, highlights, and notes to yourself all over. That's perfectly fine and completely normal for a work in progress. In fact, masterworks may have blanks, too. This is how the spreadsheet helps you to identify areas where you could tell a better story.

There is one more important step to keep in mind for works in progress. *Don't fix!* As tempting as it can be, it's important to resist the urge to start fixing things while you're working through the spreadsheet. The fixing step will come later after you've evaluated what you've found. When the time comes, it's common to find solutions that solve multiple issues. For example, a macro-level change might make some micro fixes irrelevant. Do yourself a favor and *complete* the spreadsheet before you make changes to your story. There's no need to create more work for yourself. Trust the process.

Now, it's time to evaluate what you found and decide how you want to use those insights. As you look closely at what you've uncovered, you will start to see connections: the way each piece of information contributes to the scene and the way each scene contributes to the story. In a masterwork, this can inform and inspire your own choices in your writing. You can note what you liked that worked well or even what you didn't like that you would do differently. In a work in progress, you can evaluate what exists and what is missing, what is working and what needs work. These insights become your to-do list for revisions.

Let's take a closer look at how to interpret the spreadsheet, and then I'll show you how to apply what you find to your own work.

LAYERS AND LENSES OF INSIGHT

A repeating pattern of threes can be found throughout the principles of Story.

The structure of beginning hook, middle build, and ending payoff.

The modes of narrative drive: suspense, mystery, and dramatic irony.

The types of conflict: internal, interpersonal, and extrapersonal.

We find a similar pattern when analyzing scenes. We can look at them at three different levels of analysis:

- Within one scene
- Between two or more scenes in a sequence or quadrant
- Within the whole of the story

ANALYZING A SINGLE SCENE

With this lens, we are looking at a single scene to see if it's working. This means each cell is not only complete but contains the information that is the best fit for the scene.

You were very careful when filling in the spreadsheet to ensure that everything you entered was actually on the page. Now, when you go back and analyze your results, you can identify those places where the details you hoped to find were not on the page. This is what you'll be tackling in revisions.

Analytical Constraints or Tracking the Global Story

- Word Count/Story Event: Do the number of words match the importance of the events that take place and the level of detail the reader needs?

Change

- Value Shift: Did you find a value shift? Evaluate whether this on-the-page value shift is effective for the intended purpose of the scene and Story Event. Do you need to add more on the page to ensure the shift you intended is felt by the reader?
- Turning Point: Is there a turning point? Note if the turning point directly relates to the value shift you documented. Could these two items align more directly, and would that make the scene stronger?

Continuity

- Point of View: Is there a clear and distinct point of view in the scene, or is it muddled? If there are moments when the point of view slips into something else, determine whether it's intentional.
- Period/Time: Are there indicators of period/time on the page? Evaluate whether they

communicate at the level the story needs. Are they too overt or covert for the reader?

- Duration: Are there indicators of duration on the page? Evaluate their accuracy, given the events that take place. Are they too overt or covert for the reader?
- Location: Are there sufficient details on the page to indicate location? Are there clear transitions when the location changes?
- Ultimately, for Continuity, will the reader be confused by any of the information pertaining to these categories in the scene?

Characters

- Onstage Characters: How does each character contribute to the scene? Is any character unnecessary?
- Offstage Characters: How does each character contribute to the scene? Is any character unnecessary?

You'll notice not all the columns have been addressed with the scene-level lens. For some columns, we can only determine if the information is the best fit by looking at the scene in the broader context of the sequence or global story.

ANALYZING A SEQUENCE OF SCENES

When we analyze a sequence or quadrant, we look at how each individual scene functions in the context of the scenes around it as well as any patterns that appear within the group.

Analytical Constraints or Tracking the Global Story

- Word Count: How does the word count of the scene compare to the scenes around it? If it is substantially larger or smaller, is there a relevant story-related reason?
- Word Count/Story Event: Like with the scene-level analysis, compare the total word count for the sequence or quadrant to the progression of Story Events. Does it correlate? Is the story progressing as needed to create narrative drive for the reader? Is the pace too fast or too slow?

Change

- Polarity Shift: Does the direction vary (-/--, -/+, +/-, +/++) from scene to scene or is it repetitive?
- Turning Point: Does the type (active or revelatory) vary from scene to scene or is it repetitive?

Characters

- Number of Onstage Characters: Is there variety or is it repetitive?

ANALYZING THE FULL LIST OF SCENES

For this level of analysis, we zoom all the way out and assess all the scenes together as well as the context of a single scene within the whole.

Analytical Constraints or Tracking the Global Story

- Scene Number and Story Event: Use this to get an idea of the global timing of story events.
- Word Count: What is the total word count for the story? Is the word count for each quadrant (Beginning

Hook, Middle Build 1, Middle Build 2, Ending Payoff) proportionate?

Change

- Value Shift and Turning Point: How does this scene change affect the global change?

Continuity

- Point of View: Look at the entries within this column to see if the story has more than one point of view, and notice the timing of shifts. How often does it change? How many scenes and words are given to each? Evaluate whether the rhythm and proportion make sense for the story and the experience the reader needs.
- Period/Time and Duration: How much time passes in the entire story? Does it correlate to the scope of events that happen in the story? Assess if too much or not enough time passes. For example, if a character gets pregnant, carries to term, and delivers, does enough time pass in your story for that to be

believable? To find the total duration of the story, compare the period/time when the story begins to when the story ends. How much time has passed? Does this correlate to the time passed in the Duration column?

Characters

- Onstage Characters and Offstage Characters: Look at when characters are introduced, both onstage and offstage, paying close attention to the opening scene and opening sequence. Consider how character appearances are distributed across the quadrants (Beginning Hook, Middle Build 1, Middle Build 2, Ending Payoff). Determine if these introductions are serving the story. Would it be beneficial for the character to be introduced earlier or later?
- Number of Onstage Characters and Number of Offstage Characters: Look at the number of characters introduced in the opening scene. Is it feasible for the reader to process and connect with this number of

characters at this point in the story?

- Onstage Characters and Offstage Characters: Follow each character's progression through the story. How many times do they appear? Does anyone only appear once, either onstage or offstage? Note each character's final appearance and how that timing serves the story. Does anyone drop out of the story or go unmentioned for a significant stretch of time? Are the characters set up and paid off in a satisfying way?

With this information for each scene, you can use other tools, like the Foolscap Global Story Grid and the Story Grid Infographic, for further analysis. These tools help you zoom out to look at each of your units of story from other angles.

APPLYING YOUR INSIGHTS

Now that you have completed the spreadsheet and analyzed it from all three vantage points, you are ready to culminate your findings.

Masterwork

If you have analyzed a masterwork, you have immersed at the ground level and observed what makes the story tick. Make a list of insights about each category. What choices did the author make? What impact do those choices have on the story? What experience do they create for the reader? What do you think the author's choices say about their intention for the story? Do you like the choices or not? How would you apply these insights to your own story?

Work in Progress

If you've made a spreadsheet for your own work in progress, you have identified if anything is missing or not quite right for your story. Now, you can get ready to address the issues you've found by aggregating them into a list so you can determine the best solutions.

Based on your analysis of the spreadsheet, make a list of problems to solve. Consider identifying global-level problems first, followed by sequence/quadrant-problems, and then scene-level problems.

Then, consider what changes you could make to address the issues you've found. It may take time to discover the best solution, so don't be in a rush. In fact, this is a great time to set your project aside and take in masterworks for the various aspects of your story that you are trying to improve. You will get a break from grinding on your own story and get inspired by the storytellers you love. When the time comes to revise, work from the largest to smallest unit of story, making global-level changes first and working down to the scene level.

7

DIGGING DEEPER TO LEVEL UP
EVEN MORE

Now that you've completed your first Story Grid Spreadsheet, you understand the basics. Continue improving your craft by making more. Keep in mind there is no rule that says a spreadsheet has to be all or nothing. Depending on what you're seeking to understand at that moment, you may choose to break down some or all of a story—perhaps the opening scene, or the climax, or the muddy middle. You get to decide. The more you use this tool, the more insights you will unlock.

To learn more and practice your spreadsheet skills, check out the following resources.

WATCH THE SPREADSHEET COURSE

I created a ten-lesson video course that walks you through completing the spreadsheet with practical step-by-step application. It includes three real-time examples of reading, finding, and filling, using two scenes from published masterworks and one from my own work in progress. The course is especially great for visual learners!

https://storygrid.lpages.co/spreadsheet-foundations-sales-page/

READ A MASTERWORK GUIDE

Story Grid Publishing has issued a variety of Masterwork Guides. They analyze masterworks in different genres scene by scene and provide global overviews. Each one has a completed Story Grid Spreadsheet, Foolscap, and Infographic to demonstrate how the story is working.

Using a Masterwork Guide to study presents a valuable opportunity. You can analyze the featured story yourself and check your work against the findings of the guide's author. The best part? More titles are being issued all the time.

https://storygrid.com/books/

WORK WITH AN EDITOR

A great way to get specific, personal, one-on-one feedback about your story and your spreadsheet is to hire one of the Story Grid Certified Editors. They can guide you through completing your spreadsheet and making a plan for revisions.

https://storygrid.com/editing/

8

EMBRACING THE MESS

Keep in mind that the Story Grid Spreadsheet is a living document. It grows alongside you. As you level up your craft, your spreadsheet will likely face many revisions and refinements.

On a Q&A episode of the Story Grid Podcast, someone asked Shawn, "How do you know if what you're tracking is a big beat or a small scene?"

He answered, "How many rows do you want on your spreadsheet?"

The point is there are no explicit right or wrong answers here—only what you deem best for your purposes. Your job is to roll up your sleeves to dig in and figure out what that is. Use what you know about Story to find your interpretation of the scenes and track it as best as you can.

Don't worry if your data isn't perfect—because it won't be.

This is good news!

Perfect was never the point.

The spreadsheet is akin to a painter's palette, a chef's knife, or an architect's scratchpad—tools to be used, not admired. Tools get messy. It's an expected part of the process. You clean them up when you're *done*. Yes, we will always strive to abide by the principles that make stories powerful for our audience, but that does not mean we—or our stories—are rigid machines. Neither is the Story Grid Spreadsheet. Go easy on yourself and don't worry if your spreadsheet has blanks and highlights and notes to yourself. In fact, I encourage it. Let go of perfect and simply embrace being curious nerds who love Story.

The amazing thing about the Story Grid Spreadsheet is that there is immense value in simply completing it. The process of reading, finding, and filling teaches you how to see the critical details that make a story work on the ground level. Take notes, get messy, and follow where the process leads you. Even if you decide not to take your analysis any further, the benefits you gain just from filling it in are worth it.

Whatever part of the writing process you're in, don't let the pressure of "doing it right" or the fear of "doing it wrong" keep you from doing it. Instead, lean in with boldness and love for your craft, your story, your reader, and yourself.

When you do that, you have nothing to fear, simply new connections to make.

ABOUT THE AUTHOR

KIMBERLY KESSLER is a Story Grid Certified Editor, TEDx speaker, and contributor to the *Story Grid Editor Roundtable* podcast. As an editor, she specializes in crafting authentic character arcs and internally driven stories. As a novelist and filmmaker, she uses humor as a means to cope with and explore trauma—ultimately, so we can find a redemptive perspective on pain. She lives in Washington state with her stand-up comedian husband and three "think they're a comedian" kids. You can connect with her directly at kimberkessler.com.

ABOUT THE EDITOR

DANIELLE KIOWSKI is a Story Grid Certified Editor based in Las Vegas, Nevada. She grew up with her nose in a book and loves a good story, especially if it's set in a world of urban fantasy or magical realism. As an editor, Danielle is dedicated to empowering ambitious professionals to fulfill their dreams of becoming authors by supporting their development of sustainable and productive writing practices. She believes that Story is a fundamental building block of the human experience, and that everyone, regardless of their chosen profession, can lead a more meaningful life by engaging with narrative. You can find her online at daniellekiowski.com and writersbynight.com.

Made in the USA
Columbia, SC
27 May 2021

38581790R10043